Everything You Need to Know About | *Growing Up Female*

Puberty is a time of confusing and exciting physical and emotional changes. This book will help you understand and celebrate becoming a woman.

Everything You Need to Know About *Growing Up Female*

Ellen Kahaner

The Rosen Publishing Group, Inc.
New York

Published in 1991, 1997, 2001 by The Rosen Publishing Group, Inc.
29 East 21st Street, New York, New York 10010

Copyright © 1991, 1997, 2001 by The Rosen Publishing Group, Inc.

Revised Edition 2001

All rights reserved. No part of this book may be reproduced in any form without permission in writing from the publisher, except by a reviewer.

Library of Congress Cataloging-in-Publication Data

Kahaner, Ellen.
Everything you need to know about growing up female / Ellen Kahaner.—Rev. ed.
(The need to know library)
Includes bibliographical references and index.
Summary: Discusses the changes that occur during female adolescence.
ISBN 978-1-4358-8780-0
1. Teenage girls—United States—Juvenile literature. 2. Young women—United States—Juvenile literature. 3. Puberty—United States—Juvenile literature. [1. Adolescent girls. 2. Puberty. 3. Sex instruction for girls.] I. Title. II. Series.
H0786.K27 1991
305.23'5—dc20
                                                                              90-27470
                                                                                  CIP
                                                                                   AC

Manufactured in the United States of America

Contents

	Introduction	6
Chapter 1	Growing Up Means Changing	8
Chapter 2	Your Changing Body	13
Chapter 3	Understanding the Menstrual Cycle	20
Chapter 4	Sex and Pregnancy	32
Chapter 5	Growing Up Fit	42
Chapter 6	Liking What You See in the Mirror	45
Chapter 7	Friendship and Dating	53
Chapter 8	Looking Ahead	56
	Glossary	59
	Where to Go for Help	60
	For Further Reading	62
	Index	63

Introduction

We grow and change throughout our lives. The period in which many of the greatest changes take place is during adolescence—the period of life from puberty to maturity. This book will discuss the growing process that females go through during adolescence.

Growing up means different things to different people. Some think of it as becoming more mature, free, and responsible. They look forward to being an adult, or being old enough to wear makeup, date, drive, or vote. But to others, growing up may also seem frightening, because growing means changing. All of a sudden, your body begins to look different as it prepares you for adulthood. You also experience new feelings and you may begin to feel very self-conscious about the way you look.

As you grow up, you are able to engage in more adult activities, such as wearing makeup.

This book will explain what young women can expect during this time of change. You will learn about your developing body and how to keep it healthy. You will also learn about dating and sex and how to protect yourself from pregnancy and sexually transmitted diseases (STDs). Although the changes of adolescence can sometimes make you feel confused or anxious, understanding why they occur usually makes them easier to handle.

Your teen years are an exciting time when you begin to make choices about your future and consider the direction you want your life to take. In this period of self-discovery, you will begin to think independently, developing your own ideas, style, and goals.

Chapter 1: Growing Up Means Changing

Michelle

"Anne and I have been best friends since we were kids. We used to do everything together. I just assumed it would stay that way forever. But lately Anne doesn't want to hang out anymore. We were never popular, but we didn't care because we had each other. We didn't need anyone else. We never used to be into clothes or looks or boys or anything. But now Anne has started wearing makeup and reading fashion magazines. She hangs out with the popular girls and flirts with the jocks. If she sees me in the hallway she looks away and seems embarrassed. What's the deal? What happened to my best friend? I miss her. I feel like I don't know her anymore, like she's a stranger. Now I feel totally alone."

As you get older, you may find yourself growing apart from your childhood friends.

Changes that occur as you are growing up can be difficult to understand. Some of your friends may start doing things that seem strange to you. Or maybe you're the one who is acting differently. This is all normal. The years between the ages of nine and sixteen are known as puberty. During these years you will experience dramatic changes: physically, emotionally, and psychologically.

You are changing, inside and out. You may be experiencing new emotions. Your emotions change partly because of what is happening inside your body. The people around you affect your feelings, too. For example,

Growing Up Female

you may feel angry at your parents for not giving you more freedom to make your own choices.

As you grow up, you will also go through psychological changes that affect your personality—who you are based on what you think, what is important to you, and how you behave. You may begin to look at the world in different and new ways. Ideas and things that were once important to you may now seem silly and childish. Or you may find yourself thinking about things that you never used to pay much attention to, like boys. As you change, the people around you may begin to treat you differently. Have your parents begun to ask you to take on more responsibility around the house?

You may feel alone as you go through all these changes, but you're not. Everyone goes through changes during puberty. But each person reacts to change in her own way.

Chandra

"This year, all of my friends have suddenly become women. Their breasts have gotten bigger, they have hips, they're shaving their legs. But I'm still a beanpole. I know it will happen to me someday too, but sometimes I feel like it never will. I feel sort of left out, like I'm still a kid and my friends are all way ahead of me. Some of them say they hate how their bodies have changed. They feel too big and don't like the stares they're starting to get from boys.

Growing Up Means Changing

They say I'm lucky to still be so skinny. But I want curves too! I don't want to be left behind."

The changes in your body during puberty are dramatic. People change at different rates and ages. For example, the average age at which girls start menstruating (having their period) is twelve or thirteen. But some girls start to menstruate as early as eight or as late as seventeen.

Carmen

"Sometimes I still feel like playing with dolls with my younger sister or watching Saturday morning cartoons or playing hide and seek with the neighborhood kids. But when I'm with my school friends, those kinds of things embarrass me. Then I don't want to be a kid anymore. I want to hang out with my girlfriends and talk about cool stuff, like movies and music. It's really confusing. It's like I live in two different worlds."

As you grow up, you will occasionally experience conflicting emotions. You may want to be treated differently. But sometimes you also want to be treated the same as always. How do you handle all of these emotions? One way is to share your feelings with your friends. It helps to know that someone understands how you feel. A friend can make a big difference.

Growing Up Female

Growing up is a psychological change. Your personality is affected by what happens to you in your family and in the world around you. What happens to you now—at home, at school, with friends, and on dates—will help to shape the person you are becoming. It is natural to want to lead your own life and work towards personal goals. You need to think seriously about your own values and interests. The decisions you make during adolescence play an important role in shaping your life as an adult.

Chapter 2

Your Changing Body

Shanice

"I used to be called a shrimp. I was one of the shortest kids in my class, but this year, all of a sudden, I shot up like a weed. I must have grown at least four inches. I'm also gaining a lot of weight. I used to be able to eat all kinds of junk and stay really skinny, but now my hips and legs are getting bigger. Even my feet are getting huge. None of my clothes fit anymore. I'm almost a foot taller than most of the boys in my class. I feel like a freak, a really awkward freak."

The rapid growth that you experience during puberty is called a growth spurt. In sixth or seventh grade you may begin to notice that most of the girls

Growth spurts during puberty can make you feel awkward.

are taller than the boys. That's because girls get their growth spurt—the first sign of puberty—at about the age of ten and boys don't get theirs until a couple of years later. Before puberty, both boys and girls grow about two inches a year. But once puberty hits, you can grow as much as four inches a year at the peak of the spurt, which is usually about two years after it begins. By the time you get your first menstrual period, your growing will probably have slowed down. By the second or third year after your first period, you will probably have stopped growing completely, though it is possible to grow another inch or two up to the age of twenty-one or so.

Your Changing Body

Boys will catch up in a couple of years. By the time you are thirteen or fourteen, many of the boys will be taller than the girls again. On average, boys don't begin puberty until they are in their mid- to late teens.

A New You

Growing taller is only one of many changes that occur during the growth spurt and puberty. But what makes puberty start in the first place? Sometime between the ages of eight and fourteen, special glands in your brain (called the pituitary and hypothalamus glands) start to send a new signal to your ovaries (the reproductive organs that hold all the eggs you were born with). This signal tells your ovaries to increase production of the female sex hormones estrogen and progesterone. It is the increase in these two hormones that triggers all of the changes in your body during puberty.

And there are a lot of changes that take place in just a few years. Overall, your body will become curvier. This is mainly because your hips and thighs will broaden and your pelvis will expand. Your body fat is rearranged during puberty, so that new fat tissue grows around your abdomen, hips, thighs, and buttocks. This is your body's way of getting ready for pregnancy. This is a normal and healthy process; it does not mean you are getting fat. To carry a baby

Growing Up Female

someday, your body needs to be more solid in the middle than it was when you were a kid.

Your breasts will also begin to get bigger. The area right around your nipples grows first, and then the rest of your breasts will grow too. They will continue to get bigger and rounder until you are eighteen or so. You may worry that your breasts are too large or too small. It's not a good idea to compare yourself to others because each girl's rate of growth and size is different.

While your hips and breasts are filling out, your face will probably become thinner. Your features will become more distinct and adultlike as the bones in your face change. Your feet will grow faster than the rest of your body, including your arms and legs. This may make you feel a little awkward, as if you're always tripping over your own feet. But don't worry; the rest of your body will soon catch up.

Puberty also causes hair to grow in new places, such as around your genital area (your private parts). About a year after this hair appears, you will also begin to notice hair under your arms. At the same time, the hair on your legs will grow thicker and may become darker. The hair on your arms may also darken.

You will also notice that you begin to sweat more during your teenage years and that the sweat has more of an odor than it used to have. This is because your sweat glands are more active. You can avoid

Your Changing Body

body odor by showering often and by using a deodorant or an antiperspirant.

The oil glands in your body are also more active during adolescence. Overly active oil glands can cause skin problems. Pimples, blackheads, and whiteheads form when oil is trapped in the pores of your skin. They are symptoms of a very common skin condition called acne. Acne occurs in three out of four teenagers. It can usually be treated with nonprescription products. But in serious cases, acne may need to be treated by a doctor.

Perhaps the most important development during puberty is the beginning of your menstrual cycle, which indicates that it is now possible for you to become pregnant. You are physically capable of having a baby. Your first period usually comes soon after your breasts and pubic hair begin to develop. At this time your vagina, uterus, and ovaries will begin to grow.

About six months to a year before your first period you may notice a small amount of a clear, milky, white liquid coming from your vagina. This is perfectly normal and nothing to worry about. Once you get regular periods, this vaginal discharge will often occur just before ovulation (ovulation is when your body releases an egg, which occurs roughly two weeks before your period begins). It may make you feel more comfortable to wear a pantiliner when this happens.

Your friends may mature faster or slower than you do. Everyone grows up in her own unique way.

Everyone's on Her Own Schedule

All of these physical changes affect how you feel about yourself. You may feel like you no longer recognize your body. You may suddenly feel big and awkward. Talking to your friends about what is happening will help you feel better. Together you can discuss how your bodies are changing and how that makes you all feel. You will realize that you are all experiencing the same sort of confusing, exciting, frightening changes and can support each other through this difficult time.

Your Changing Body

Or you may be worried because your body hasn't started to change yet although your friends' have. Every girl is different and will develop at her own rate. In addition, sometimes extremely athletic girls, such as gymnasts, experience a late puberty. If you are worried that you are developing slowly or late, consider talking to your mother about when she went through puberty. Chances are you will begin puberty at about the same time she did. But don't worry; it will happen.

As confusing as puberty can be, it is a very exciting time too. It marks the threshold to adulthood and greater maturity and responsibility. You are becoming a woman, and that is really something to celebrate!

Chapter 3
Understanding the Menstrual Cycle

The beginning of menstruation is one of the most dramatic changes that young women experience during puberty. Menstruation is also referred to as getting your period. From the time when a young woman experiences her first menstrual cycle, she is physically capable of becoming pregnant and having a baby.

For most women, the menstrual cycle takes about twenty-eight days, but it can vary from twenty-one to forty days. Most young women get their first period between the ages of eleven and fourteen, though it can also first occur in girls as young as eight or as old as seventeen. This entire range is normal. If you are sixteen, however, and haven't gotten your first period yet, see a doctor. You may have a hormonal imbalance

Understanding the Menstrual Cycle

which can be corrected. In general, your period will probably begin about two years after your breasts first begin to develop.

The Start of Menstruation

When a girl first begins to menstruate, the cycle may not be regular. This means that you may or may not have your period at the same time every month, and you may even skip months. In the first few years of menstruation, you might get more than one period a month or no period at all for a few months. This irregular pattern can cause some problems because your period can come when you least expect it. One way to deal with this is to always carry pads or tampons with you. You should begin to do this as soon as your body begins to change so that when your first period comes you won't be caught by surprise. In some cases, a woman may never get on a regular, predictable cycle. But chances are you will begin to follow a regular schedule after a few months or a year.

Some young women have never had an opportunity to learn about the menstrual cycle because they and their parents are embarrassed to talk about it. As a result, they don't know what to do when they first begin menstruating. If you're confused and feel uncomfortable talking to your parents about it, there

Whether you decide to use tampons or pads—or both—is up to you.

Understanding the Menstrual Cycle

are many people who can answer your questions or just talk about teen issues. An older sister, an aunt, a school nurse, or a teacher can help you understand your period.

The Menstrual Cycle

Your menstrual cycle begins the first day of your period (when you begin menstruating, or bleeding) and ends the first day of flow of your next period. The cycle usually lasts twenty-eight days.

Your menstrual cycle has two purposes: to prepare your uterus for a fetus (unborn baby) to grow in if you become pregnant, and to clean out the uterus if pregnancy does not occur.

The following is a list of the body organs that are part of the menstrual cycle and reproductive process:

- **Cervix: lower, narrow end of the uterus that juts into the vagina.**
- **Fallopian tubes: two tubes on top of the uterus that carry one ripe egg from an ovary to the uterus each month.**
- **Follicle: a tiny pocket in the ovary where an egg ripens.**
- **Hormones: chemical substances that travel in your blood and tell your body's organs**

If you are uncomfortable talking to your parents about your body, seek the advice of a trusted adult or friend.

how to develop. Your body makes hundreds of hormones. Estrogen and progesterone are the hormones that affect the menstrual cycle.

- **Ovaries:** two organs that provide safe storage for the thousands of eggs you were born with. Each ovary is about the size and shape of an almond.

- **Uterus:** hollow organ where a fetus develops. The uterus grows during puberty to the size of a fist. It can expand to many times its size to accommodate a baby.

Understanding the Menstrual Cycle

About a week after your menstrual cycle begins, the ovaries send out a hormone called estrogen, which causes the lining of your uterus to become thick with blood and tissue. This prepares your uterus for pregnancy.

Around the fourteenth day of the menstrual cycle, a process called ovulation occurs. A single ripe egg breaks out of its follicle and moves into the fallopian tube. You may feel a twinge or cramp in your lower abdomen or back during ovulation.

The egg moves through the fallopian tube to the uterus. Meanwhile, the broken follicle from which the egg emerged secretes the hormones estrogen and progesterone. These hormones cause the uterine lining to become even thicker. If the egg is not fertilized by a sperm (if you do not become pregnant), the egg breaks down. The lining of the uterus starts to shed by about day twenty-four.

By day twenty-eight, the uterine lining has loosened so much that it breaks off and begins to come out of your vagina. The beginning of menstruation is called day one of your next menstrual cycle.

What comes out of your vagina is usually called blood because it is red. But it is really a mixture of tissue, mucus, and blood shed from the lining of the uterus. Some blood is lost, but not much.

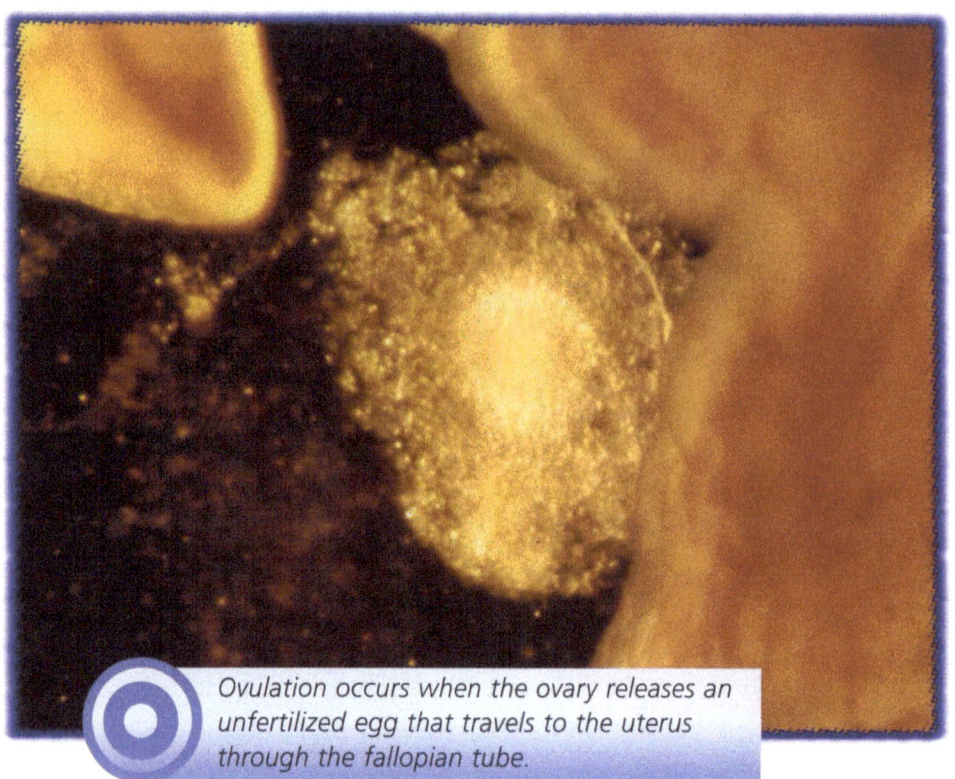

Ovulation occurs when the ovary releases an unfertilized egg that travels to the uterus through the fallopian tube.

Period Symptoms

During periods, women may experience some discomfort, such as bloating, tender breasts, backaches, and cramps. Cramps are caused by muscles in your uterus that tighten up to push the menstrual fluid out. Some women also experience headaches, fatigue (tiredness), sudden emotional changes, and a greater amount of oil on their face (which may cause acne breakouts). These are symptoms of a menstrual period and are normal. They are similar to the symptoms of PMS (premenstrual syndrome), which will be discussed later in this chapter.

Understanding the Menstrual Cycle

Not all young women experience menstruation in the same way. That is because each woman's body works differently. For example, some women have cramps with every period, while others never have cramps. The level of discomfort can also vary. Menstrual bleeding may last for only two or three days or up to a week or longer. Some women have a heavy flow (they bleed a lot) for a day or two and a lighter flow for a few other days. Others bleed very little.

Most women do not change their daily activities when they have their periods. They go to school or work, exercise, and play sports. Exercise can help to lessen cramps and make you feel better. But others experience such bad cramps that they may need to stay in bed. Those who experience severe symptoms should see a doctor. A doctor who specializes in women's reproductive health is called a gynecologist.

Premenstrual Syndrome

PMS is a combination of emotional and physical changes that you may go through before your period. It is not the same as the discomfort of the cramps and bleeding you feel during your period. Most researchers and doctors believe it is caused by the hormonal changes that occur during the menstrual cycle. Sometimes the symptoms of PMS are mild, but sometimes they are so severe they can begin to affect a woman's performance at work or school and her personal relationships. The most common symptoms are:

- Depression, feelings of helplessness, anxiety, and tension
- Sudden and dramatic mood swings marked by anger and irritability
- Less interest in the things you like to do
- Difficulty concentrating
- Lack of energy, tiredness
- Food cravings, especially for something sweet or salty
- Difficulty sleeping
- Breast tenderness, headaches, joint and muscle aches, bloating, and weight gain
- Oily skin and hair

For some women, the symptoms last for only a day or two before their period begins. Other women experience PMS from just after ovulation until the start of the period. Only 2 to 5 percent of women suffer from severe PMS, and many women have only a few or mild symptoms. Some women don't have any of these symptoms or only experience them occasionally. PMS is most commonly experienced by women in their

Understanding the Menstrual Cycle

twenties and thirties, and PMS symptoms disappear entirely after menopause.

There are several things you can do to help reduce PMS symptoms. Avoiding caffeine and alcohol, reducing salt intake, and drinking lots of water have helped many women with their mood swings, anxiety, fatigue, and bloating. Aerobic exercise is also thought to help with your mood. Exercise seems to stimulate chemicals in your brain that produce a kind of natural high, increasing your sense of well-being and relaxation. A hot bath or a heating pad can help relieve your cramps, as can a gentle abdomen massage. Make sure you get enough sleep. Being tired and in pain is a bad combination that makes it much harder to cope. If necessary, an over-the-counter painkiller like ibuprofen should help reduce your pain. These work best if taken just before and during your period. If your symptoms are severe and hampering your school and family life, a doctor may prescribe various medications to help you feel better.

What Do I Use When I Have My Period?

Young women today have many choices for dealing with their periods. Information about these choices is available from several sources. There are advertisements in magazines and on television for products to use when

Growing Up Female

you have your period. Your mother, friend, or school nurse can also help you decide what's best for you.

Menstrual pads, sometimes referred to as sanitary napkins, are made of paper and other absorbent fibers. Most pads have adhesive strips that attach directly to your underwear. They have a fluidproof shield inside that protects against leaking and staining. Pads come in many sizes and shapes. Some are thick to protect against a heavy flow. These are often called maxi-pads by the companies that make them. Some pads are very thin and can be used toward the end of your period or when you think you might get your period. These are often called mini-pads or panty shields. You may want to try different shapes and sizes of pads until you find the one that suits your needs.

The other kind of protection that you can use during your period is called a tampon. Tampons are worn inside your body. A tampon is made of paper and other absorbent fibers rolled together in the shape of a tube. These fibers absorb the menstrual flow. Some tampons have a plastic or cardboard applicator that makes them easier to insert into the vagina. A tampon has a string attached to it. A portion of the string hangs down just below the lips of the vagina for removal of the tampon.

A very important thing to remember about tampons is that you must change them often, at least two or three

Understanding the Menstrual Cycle

times a day. A very serious disease called toxic shock syndrome (TSS) can be caused by not changing tampons frequently enough. TSS is a rare disease, but it can be deadly. Your chances of getting TSS increase if you use tampons, especially if you don't change them frequently. Some research indicates that the more absorbent the tampon, the higher the risk of contracting TSS. So if you don't have a heavy flow, consider buying a regular rather than a super-absorbency tampon.

Keep in mind that TSS is a rare disease; less than one-fifth of one percent of menstruating women ever get it. Its symptoms include vomiting, diarrhea, dizziness and fainting, weakness, aching muscles and joints, fever, red eyes, sore throat, and a rash. If you notice any of these symptoms and you are wearing a tampon, remove it immediately and do not insert a new one. Call your doctor right away. But you should feel perfectly safe using tampons as long as you follow the package directions for insertion, removal, and regular changing.

Whatever you decide to use when you have your period, remember to change the product frequently. This is important for your health and will make you feel cleaner.

Chapter 4 | Sex and Pregnancy

As you have learned in the previous chapter, a woman is capable of becoming pregnant from the time she experiences her first menstrual cycle. This doesn't mean that she has to, or wants to, or is emotionally ready to have a baby. It simply means that she has the potential to become pregnant.

You can become pregnant if you have sex during ovulation, or shortly before or after. This also holds true for your very first menstrual cycle. About two weeks before your first period begins, your ovary will release an egg. This means that a young woman can become pregnant during her first menstrual cycle just

Sex and Pregnancy

before she experiences her first menstruation. So just because you haven't gotten your first period yet doesn't mean you can't get pregnant. You should also remember that you can ovulate at a different time each month. There are no "safe days" to have sex. If you do not want to become pregnant, you must always use some form of birth control. Keep in mind, however, that no form of birth control is 100 percent effective.

How Pregnancy Happens

When a male is sexually excited, his penis fills with blood and becomes hard. This is called an erection. It is this hardness that allows the penis to enter the vagina easily. During intercourse, semen that contains sperm is released when the muscles of the erect penis contract. The semen is forced up and out through the urethra, a tube that runs down the middle of the penis. This process is called ejaculation. When a man ejaculates, he experiences an orgasm—the climax of arousal or sexual excitement.

Millions of sperm are released each time a male ejaculates. When ejaculation occurs during sexual intercourse, the sperm swim to the top of the vagina. They pass through the cervix into the uterus. Some sperm swim into the fallopian tubes. A single sperm breaks

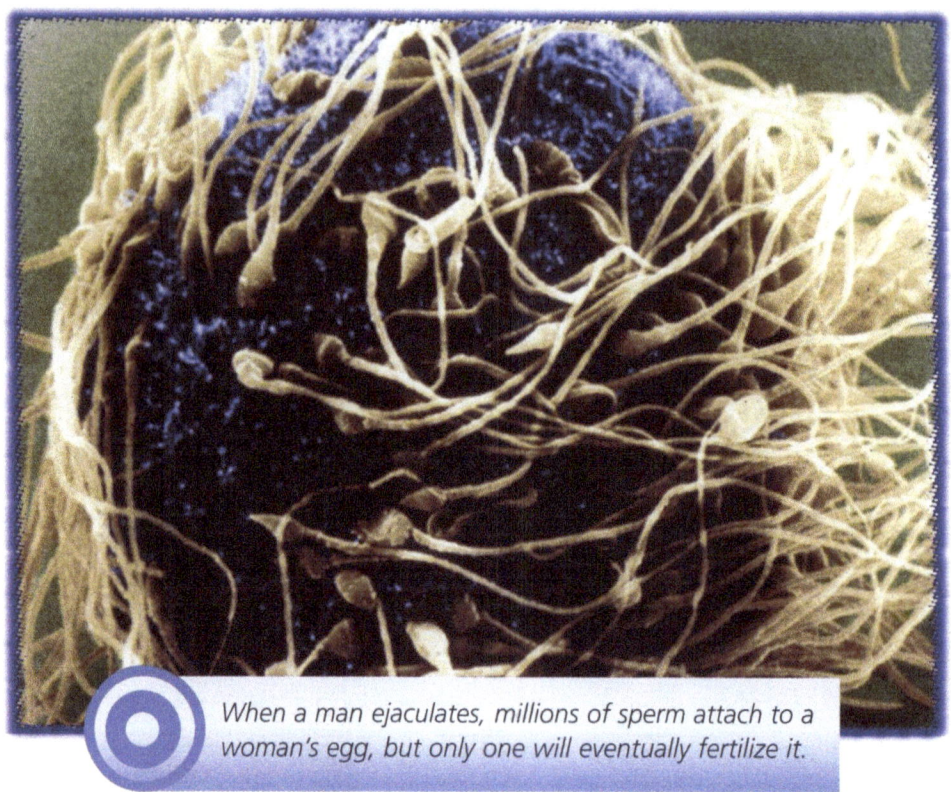

When a man ejaculates, millions of sperm attach to a woman's egg, but only one will eventually fertilize it.

through the shell of the ripe egg and moves inside it. This is called fertilization. After the egg is fertilized, it moves into the uterus. The fertilized egg then attaches itself to the wall of the uterus and pregnancy begins.

Pregnancy usually occurs during sexual intercourse. However, there is a possibility that sperm can enter the vagina without penetration and cause pregnancy. For example, pregnancy can occur if semen is released near the opening of the vagina and then drips into the vagina. It is even possible, though unlikely, for sperm to pass through fabric (such as underwear) that comes in contact with semen. Also, if fingers that have touched semen enter the vagina, pregnancy may result.

Sex and Pregnancy

Making the Right Decision for You

It's important to be informed about sex in order to make good decisions. You are the only one who can decide whether you are ready to have sex or not. You may want to remain a virgin until you get married. Or you may feel that having sex is an important part of a relationship whether you are married or not. Whatever your beliefs about sex are, make sure that they are respected by other people. Don't let yourself be pressured into sexual activity by friends or boyfriends.

It's also important to act responsibly if you choose to have sex. Being sexually responsible means not doing anything that can hurt you or your partner. It means having safer sex by using birth control to prevent pregnancy, AIDS (acquired immunodeficiency syndrome), and other STDs. Remember, too, that it isn't just your responsibility to make sure that you don't become pregnant or infected. Birth control and protection against disease are your partner's responsibility, too.

The only surefire protection against both pregnancy and STDs is abstinence (deciding not to have sex). Sometimes there is a lot of peer pressure to have sex or you may feel pressured by your boyfriend. And sometimes it seems as though everyone is having sex except for you. You should know, however, that many teenagers are choosing abstinence as a way to stay safe and healthy until they truly feel ready to have sex.

Choosing to have sex is an important decision. Make sure that you are not pressured into it.

Sex and Pregnancy

Roughly 50 percent of all unmarried women between the ages of fifteen and nineteen and 45 percent of unmarried men in the same age group have never had sex. One recent survey indicates that most teenagers, even those who are not virgins, feel that young people should wait until they are at least eighteen to twenty-one years old before they start having sex. There are even large numbers of unmarried men and women in their twenties and thirties who are choosing to hold off on sex until they meet just the right person or until they get married. So if you do choose abstinence, you are not at all alone or weird in any way.

All teenagers have some interest in sex, even if they are only curious about it. Some teenagers think about sex a lot. Others don't. They may not even be ready for dating. That is okay, too. Everyone develops at her or his own pace and has different interests and desires. It is important to think about what is right for you.

Birth Control and STDs

Birth control is easy for you to obtain if you know the facts. If you decide to have sex and do not want to become pregnant, be responsible and use birth control.

Another factor to consider when deciding to have sex is the possible transmission of sexually transmitted diseases. Each year more than 12 million Americans are infected with an STD. One out of every four of them

Growing Up Female

is a teenager. Some STDs are only an annoyance, but some can cause permanent health problems for you, your partner, and your baby (when and if you have one), and some can even result in death. Some STDs, like herpes, can be treated but never cured. Once you get it, you are never free of it, and you can infect all of your future partners and put your baby at risk for severe illness, disabilities, and even death. Some STDs, such as gonorrhea, syphilis, and chlamydia, can be cured, but can still have terrible consequences, such as infertility, brain damage, heart disease, nerve damage, and cervical cancer.

HIV (human immunodeficiency virus), the virus that causes AIDS, is an incredibly deadly virus. You may have been hearing a lot about the new drugs being used to treat AIDS. They have helped improve the quality and duration of many patients' lives, but they are not a cure. They are complicated to take, have strong side effects, and don't work for everyone. New research indicates they may stop working after someone takes them for a while. Every day people are still dying of AIDS in America and worldwide. Every year another 20,000 Americans become infected, joining the almost 900,000 people already living with HIV in this country. And don't think that teenagers who have sex with other teenagers are immune; half of all new HIV infections occur in people under the age of twenty-five.

Sex and Pregnancy

AIDS is still the leading cause of death for Americans between the ages of twenty-five and forty-four.

You've probably heard that when you have sex with someone, you're not just having sex with that person but also with everyone they've ever had sex with. It may seem like a cliché, but it's very true. So, as embarrassing as it may be, before you have sex, be sure to have a very frank conversation with your partner about each other's previous sexual experiences and any diseases you may have. If either of you have had unprotected sex before and have never been tested for an STD, you should get tested before having sex. The American Medical Association recommends that all sexually active young people (whether in steady relationships or not) get tested for STDs once a year. Remember, you can often have an STD without knowing it; the symptoms can show up months after infection.

You can also insist that your partner wear a condom. A condom is a thin rubber sheath that a man unrolls over his penis. It holds the sperm and fluid inside when he ejaculates. A condom provides good protection against both pregnancy and STDs because of the barrier it forms between you and your partner. Many condoms provide added protection against STDs because they contain a substance called spermicide that kills sperm.

Growing Up Female

There is also a female condom that offers protection against pregnancy and STDs. It is inserted into the vagina with an inner ring fitting over the cervix and an outer ring covering the labia. The female condom has a higher failure rate than the male condom. On average, one of every four women who uses the female condom becomes pregnant within a year.

Male and female condoms are the only form of birth control that also protect against STDs. If you are having sex you should always use one whether or not you are using some other form of birth control, like the Pill. If your boyfriend doesn't want to use a condom and tries to talk you into having sex without one, don't listen to him. Condoms don't kill the romance, as many guys claim, STDs do. A lot of guys claim they can "pull out" of your vagina before ejaculating. This is not an effective way of preventing pregnancy or disease because a man, especially a young man who doesn't have a lot of sexual experience, cannot always control when he ejaculates. It can often happen much faster than either of you expects. Also, semen can leak out of a man's penis before ejaculation.

And don't believe a guy when he says he can't feel anything when he wears a condom. It's just not true. The latex is so thin that a man should have plenty of sensation. Tell him he'll really feel nothing if he doesn't wear a condom, because there won't be any

Sex and Pregnancy

sex! Make it clear that "No condom, no sex!" is your rule, and it's not negotiable.

Remember too that oral sex (the kissing and licking of your partner's genitals), though it can't make you pregnant, is not safe sex. Many teenagers think they can avoid STDs and pregnancy by having oral sex instead of intercourse. According to the Centers for Disease Control, it is possible to get HIV and other STDs through oral sex. The viruses can enter your bloodstream through cuts or sores in your mouth. So if you're having oral sex you should still put a condom on the penis.

Many other forms of birth control are available, such as the diaphragm and the Pill, each designed for women's differing needs. You can get pamphlets describing all methods of birth control at Planned Parenthood centers and other family planning centers. You can also consult a doctor or visit a clinic to learn which birth control method is right for you and your partner. It is important to remember, however, that every form of birth control can fail, especially if used incorrectly. There is no such thing as safe sex; sex can only be made safer by protecting yourself against pregnancy and STDs with birth control that includes the use of a condom. The only method guaranteed to prevent pregnancy and STDs is sexual abstinence.

Chapter 5

Growing Up Fit

Today, girls know that being physically active helps keep their bodies and minds healthy. Exercise is good for practically every system in your body, including the cardiovascular system (the heart and blood vessels), the respiratory system (lungs), and the musculoskeletal system (muscles and skeleton).

Regular aerobic exercise (twenty minutes or more of continuous exercise about three times a week) causes your cardiovascular, respiratory, and musculoskeletal systems to work together more effectively. Aerobic exercise, such as running, biking, or swimming, requires an increased intake of oxygen. This is because your muscles demand more oxygen to work properly during vigorous exercise. You breathe more deeply and regularly to allow more oxygen to enter your lungs. The bloodstream then carries the oxygen from your lungs to muscles and other tissues in your body.

Exercise is essential to keep yourself healthy, and it helps you look and feel your best.

Growing Up Female

When you exercise, the heart must beat faster to pump oxygen-rich blood to your muscles. The heart, which is itself a muscle, becomes stronger with regular exercise. It increases the blood supply to your tissues, bringing oxygen and nutrients to every part of your body more quickly. Wastes produced by your cells, such as carbon dioxide, are also removed faster. That is why you usually feel better after exercising. Also, regular aerobic exercise may decrease your risk of heart disease.

Anaerobic exercise, such as weight lifting, does not usually require an increased intake of oxygen. As a result, it does not strengthen the heart in the same way that aerobic exercise does. However, activities like weight lifting do improve the health of your muscles. Strong muscles increase your ability to perform physical tasks and decrease your chances of injury. Without regular exercise your muscles become weak.

Regular exercise also helps to keep your bones healthy. It may help to prevent a disease called osteoporosis. This condition, which primarily affects older women, leads to weaker and more fragile bones.

It is very important for you to get the exercise you need to remain healthy and fit. Exercise will help to increase your strength and stamina, relieve stress and fatigue, and reduce your risk of certain diseases later in life. Above all, being healthy and fit will help you feel and look better.

Chapter 6
Liking What You See in the Mirror

Some people in American society believe that ideal beauty is best represented by a thin, tall woman wearing lots of makeup and expensive clothes. This image is shown so often in advertisements and in the media that you too may believe that it represents what real beauty is.

Many companies spend huge sums of money on advertising to persuade consumers to buy their products. This may involve paying models or famous people lots of money to be associated with their products so that their merchandise is more appealing to consumers. These companies want you to believe that buying a certain product will make you more popular or as appealing as the person in their ad. But without

Not everyone conforms to the ideal of female beauty promoted by advertisers and the media.

Liking What You See in the Mirror

healthy self-esteem, no product will be able to make you feel good about yourself.

While it may be fun at times to play around with your looks, some girls become obsessed with their appearance. It's important to ask yourself who benefits from all the time and money spent to conform to a certain image of beauty. Does this obsession help women grow as individuals?

How you present yourself should be based on what you want for yourself, not on what you think other people want from you. It may be hard, at first, to develop your own style and to feel good about your looks. But once you become comfortable with yourself, you will have the enormous satisfaction of knowing that you are entirely unique and individual, and not just another clone torn from the pages of a fashion magazine.

Diet

Nutrition is an important health issue during your teenage years when your body is growing and developing. In order for your body to develop in a healthy way, it needs energy and the proper nutrients that a balanced diet provides. The key to a balanced diet is moderation and variety.

Try to keep your junk food intake to a minimum. Every time that you go on chocolate, potato chip, or

It's important to develop your own style, one that reflects who you want to be, not what others want you to be.

cheeseburger binges, be sure to compensate with plenty of vegetables, fruit, and lean chicken and meat. Remember to get a lot of iron by eating red meat, fish, chicken, and green leafy vegetables. Getting your period every month can lead to a shortage of iron in your blood, which can make you tired and irritable and make it hard to concentrate in school. If you have especially heavy periods or are not getting enough iron, you may even develop anemia, which is a shortage of red blood cells. If you're worried that you're not getting enough iron through the food you eat, you can also take an iron supplement.

Liking What You See in the Mirror

Getting enough calcium is very important too. By the time you turn twenty, your bones will be as strong and dense as they are going to get. It's all downhill from here! It's very important to strengthen your bones as much as possible with calcium so that when you are in your seventies and eighties, your spine won't curve and your bones won't break easily. Milk, yogurt, and cheese are all great sources of calcium. If you're lactose-intolerant, you can drink lactose-free milk, take lactase pills to help you digest dairy products, or take a calcium supplement.

A lot of teenage girls skip breakfast, either because they are too busy or are dieting. This is a bad idea. Eating breakfast will give you more energy and concentration and will decrease your chances of snacking or overeating at dinner. People who skip breakfast tend to have more weight problems and less energy than those who don't.

You shouldn't get worried if you have gained some weight as a teenager. The average girl between the ages of fifteen and nineteen gains about ten pounds. If you think you need to lose weight, don't go on a crash diet. Just begin to eat more healthy foods in moderate portions and get regular exercise. Your weight will level off automatically once you stop growing and developing.

Growing Up Female

Eating Disorders

There is a difference between bad eating habits, like skipping breakfast or eating a pint of ice cream once in a while, and true eating disorders. Some young women don't have an accurate or healthy body image. It's estimated that 15 percent of young women have seriously unhealthy eating attitudes and behaviors. They may think they have to lose weight when they really don't. These teens don't eat enough to develop and grow properly. Through the media, teens may get the mistaken idea that being extremely thin makes them beautiful. Teens may begin to think that they are only attractive if they look as thin as supermodels, and they may starve themselves to fit this image.

Young women who worry so much about their weight may develop serious eating disorders such as anorexia nervosa or bulimia nervosa, which can permanently damage their bodies.

- **Anorexia Nervosa:** Anorexia nervosa is an eating disorder characterized by an abnormal and irrational fear of gaining weight and an inability to perceive one's true body weight and appearance accurately. It primarily affects women between the ages of thirteen and twenty-one. People with anorexia literally try to

Liking What You See in the Mirror

starve themselves with often fatal consequences. They will often hide food, obsessively count calories, avoid eating in public, and exercise excessively. The results are dangerous weight loss, low blood pressure, organ damage, lack of menstruation, dry and yellow skin, low body temperature, anemia, lightheadedness, body hair growth, severe heart problems, weak and brittle bones, and a shrinking of the brain. Roughly 1 percent of adolescent girls suffer from anorexia, and anywhere from 5 to 18 percent of those affected—an estimated 1,000 women a year—eventually die from starvation, cardiac arrest, or suicide.

- **Bulimia Nervosa:** Bulimia nervosa, often referred to as "binge and purge," is another eating disorder that involves a fear of becoming overweight. Bulimics gorge themselves, or overeat, and then force themselves to vomit the food they have eaten. Sometimes laxatives, diuretics, fasting, and excessive exercise are also used to purge their bodies after a binge. As with anorexia, it is mainly young women who suffer from

bulimia. Someone who binges and purges for an extended period may rupture her stomach or esophagus, have irregular periods, experience heart failure, rot her teeth, and develop swollen "chipmunk" cheeks. It is thought that 2 to 3 percent of adolescent girls become bulimic, and some studies show that up to 40 percent of college women admit to bingeing and purging.

Remember that what you eat affects your development and overall health. Educating yourself about good nutrition will help you develop good eating habits. Does your school offer nutrition classes? If not, you can visit your school or local library and check out a book on the subject. The most important lesson you can learn is how to be healthy and feel comfortable with yourself rather than being influenced by what other people say is the ideal body type.

Chapter 7

Friendship and Dating

During puberty it is common to spend time with a group of friends. Within that group, one or two friends may become very close. They may even want to start dating.

Sometimes you may be outside of a group that you want to be in. You may feel too shy to approach this group, or you may be scared of being rejected.

Keep in mind that everyone experiences feelings of loneliness, insecurity, and shyness at times. That's why going to a party with a friend is easier than going by yourself. You can help each other feel more at ease.

Dating

What happens when you meet someone you would like to get to know? Many young women believe that they

You may want to date a friend, or you may decide to keep the relationship nonromantic, or platonic.

should wait to be asked out on a date. This gives them little control over their social life.

However, many young women today feel that they don't have to follow old-fashioned ideas about the "proper" way to act. This gives them a lot more options. Everyone understands that it's not easy to ask someone out on a date. We all know what it's like to be rejected. The worst thing that will happen if you ask someone out is that he or she will say no. But at least you've tried. That takes courage. And if the person you like says yes, then you will have the chance to develop a relationship with him or her.

Friendship and Dating

Sometimes when you go out with someone, you'll find out that you don't really like him or her. You may not want to date that person again. Or you may find that you'd be more comfortable just being friends. In both of these cases, it's important to be direct with the other person about how you feel.

You may find that you like the person you're dating a lot. You may even fall in love. These relationships can last a long time. But more often, relationships during puberty are short and intense because teenagers usually aren't yet sure about what kind of partner they want. Each relationship teaches you a little about yourself and about the kind of people that are best for you.

When you are dating, the question of how far to go sexually will probably arise. Don't be pressured into doing something you're uncomfortable with or don't want to do. If you're not sure whether you want to do something, the best thing is to wait until you are certain. Try to learn as much as you can about yourself and about relating to others. That way, next time you'll know more about how to act in a relationship and what you like and dislike.

Some people begin dating before they reach their teens. Others don't date even in high school. You may feel like you're ready for dating before you have the opportunity. Your social life may take a while to get started, but don't worry—you have plenty of time.

Chapter 8: Looking Ahead

Thinking about your future can be scary partly because you don't know what to expect. How do you prepare to become an adult? One way is to plan ahead and take an active approach to your life instead of leaving your future to chance. The decisions you make in your teen years will help shape your life as an adult.

Your society, culture, or family may give you a very strong message about what is expected of you as an adult. But you are entitled to develop your own interests in life and to pursue your own dreams.

Now is the time to start thinking about your goals. If you're not sure of your goals yet, try one of the following suggestions for thinking about your future.

Looking Ahead

Think about people whom you want to be like. If the life story of an artist, an athlete, a relative, or a friend inspires you, use that person as a role model.

Try to have new experiences. Whether it is studying in a foreign country, starting a music band, or doing volunteer work, all the experiences you have add up. They give you ideas and choices that can help you figure out what you want to do. Talk about your future with some adults who have had experiences from which you can learn. Their thoughts and advice may be helpful.

Sometimes goals can seem overwhelming or unreachable. But once you learn more about your goal, you'll often find that it's not as difficult to reach as you think. Don't be afraid to try something new or to share your ideas with others. And don't back down when someone tells you that you can't or shouldn't do something "because you're a girl."

In North American society, what it means to be a woman has changed through time. Women have not always had the same rights and expectations for their lives as men. The equal rights women enjoy today were won by the efforts of women and men who were willing to fight for them in the past.

Young women can now look forward to the same opportunities in education as young men. There are also more professional opportunities available to women today than ever before.

Growing Up Female

Young women are free to shape their lives by making their own choices about the future. They can learn everything they need to know about their bodies and how to keep themselves healthy and fit. They can decide when they are ready to have sex and when to have children. And young women can choose the career they want to pursue.

Women around the world have made much progress in the last century, and their standing in society has improved. However, there is room for further improvement, and more work to be done.

As we enter the new millennium, women can look forward to facing new challenges, as well as ever-greater possibilities. They will continue to fight to expand women's rights and improve their opportunities. Women will also continue to make important contributions to society as a whole. You will be part of the new generation that will lead the way into this exciting future and set the standard for other young women around the world.

Glossary

birth control Methods for preventing pregnancy.
hormones Chemical substances that travel in your blood and tell your body's organs how to develop.
menstrual cycle A twenty-eight-day cycle that includes menstruation (bleeding), the release of special hormones, the thickening of the uterine lining, ovulation, and the breakdown of the uterine lining.
ovaries Female reproductive organs that contain all of the eggs a woman is born with.
ovulation The process by which a ripe egg breaks out of its follicle and rises to the top of the ovary.
puberty The period between the ages of nine and sixteen when girls and boys mature physically.
uterus Hollow organ within which a fetus develops during pregnancy.

Where to Go for Help

Eating Disorders Awareness and Prevention
603 Stewart Street, Suite 803
Seattle, WA 98101
(206) 382-3587
(800) 931-2237
Web site: http://www.edap.org

iemily.com
Web site: http://www.iemily.com
This is a health and wellness Web site just for young women. It provides information on your changing body, fitness, nutrition, friends, relationships, etc.

National Organization for Women
733 15th Street NW, 2nd floor
Washington, DC 20005

Where to Go for Help

(202) 628-8669
e-mail: now@now.org
Web site: http://www.now.org

Planned Parenthood Federation of America
810 Seventh Avenue
New York, NY 10019
(212) 541-7800
e-mail: communications@ppfa.org
Web site: http://www.plannedparenthood.org

In Canada

Eating Disorder Education Organization (EDEO)
6R20 Edmonton General Hospital
11111 Jasper Avenue
Edmonton, AB T5K 0L6
(780) 944-2864
e-mail: info@edeo.org
Web site: http://www.edeo.org

Planned Parenthood Federation of Canada
1 Nicholas Street, Suite 430
Ottawa, ON K1N 7B7
(613) 241-4474
e-mail: admin@ppfc.ca
Web site: http://www.ppfc.ca

For Further Reading

Brady, Janis, Ph.D. *Your Body: The Girls' Guide*. New York: St. Martins, 2000.

Jukes, Mavis. *Growing Up: It's a Girl Thing: Straight Talk about First Bras, First Periods, and Your Changing Body*. New York: Knopf, 1998.

Madaras, Lynda, and Area Madaras. *My Feelings, My Self*. New York: Newmarket Press, 1993.

Mahoney, Ellen Voelckers. *Now You've Got Your Period*. Rev. ed. New York: The Rosen Publishing Group, Inc., 1993.

Moore, Susan, Anne Mitchell, and Doreen A. Rosenthal. *Youth, AIDS, and Sexually Transmitted Diseases*. New York: Routledge, 1996.

Mucciolo, Gary. *Everything You Need to Know About Birth Control*. Rev. ed. New York: The Rosen Publishing Group, Inc., 1998.

Index

A
abstinence, 35–37, 41
acne, 17, 26
adolescence, 6, 7, 12
anemia, 48
anorexia nervosa, 50–51
anxiety, 7, 28, 29
appearance/looks, 6, 44, 45–52

B
birth control, 33, 35, 37–41
breasts, 16, 17, 21, 26, 28
bulimia nervosa, 50, 51–52

C
calcium, 49
cervix, 23, 33, 40
changes, 9, 15
    emotional, 9–10, 11, 26
    physical, 9, 11, 15–19, 20, 27
    psychological, 9, 10, 12
chlamydia, 38
condom, importance of using, 39–41
cramps, 25, 26, 27, 29

D
dating, 6, 7, 12, 53–55
diaphragm, 41
diet, 47–48, 52

E
eating disorders, 50–52
eggs, 15, 17, 23, 25, 32, 33
ejaculation, 33, 39, 40
erection, 33
estrogen, 15, 24, 25
exercise, importance of, 29, 42–44, 49

F
fallopian tubes, 23, 25, 33
fertilization, 34
fetus, 23
follicle, 23, 25
friends, 9, 11, 12, 18, 30, 53

G
goals, your own, 7, 12, 56–58
gonorrhea, 38
growth spurt, 13–15
gynecologist, 27

H
hair growth, 16
herpes 38
HIV/AIDS, 35, 38–39
hormones, 15, 23–24, 25, 27

I
iron, 48

M
menopause, 29
menstruation/period/menstrual bleeding, 11, 14, 17, 20–23, 27, 28, 29, 48, 51, 52
   activities and, 27
   symptoms, 26–27
   irregular, 21
   menstrual cycle, 23–25, 27, 32
   pads and tampons, 21, 29–31

O
oil glands, 17, 26, 29
ovaries, 15, 17, 23, 25, 32
ovulation, 17, 25, 28, 32–33

P
parents/family, 10, 12, 19, 21, 30
penis, 33
Pill, the, 40, 41
Planned Parenthood, 41

pregnancy, 7, 15, 17, 20, 23, 25, 32–34, 35, 37, 39–40, 58
   protecting against, 35, 37–41
premenstrual syndrome (PMS), 26, 27–29
progesterone, 15, 24
puberty, 6, 9, 10, 13–19, 55
   late, 19, 20

S
sex/intercourse, 7, 32, 33–35, 35–41, 55, 58
sperm, 25, 33–34, 39, 40

U
uterine lining, 25
uterus, 17, 23, 25, 33, 34

V
vagina, 17, 23, 25, 33, 34, 40
vaginal discharge, 17

About the Author

Ellen Kahaner is a freelance writer based in New York City. She has written a number of books for young adults.

Photo Credits

Cover © Ron Chapple/FPG; p. 2 © Caroline Wood/Int'l Stock; p. 7 © Stephanie Rausser/FPG; pp. 9, 14, 18, 22, 24, 48 by Maura Boruchow; p. 26 © C. Edelmann/La Villette/Photo Researchers, Inc.; p. 34 © David M. Phillips/Science Source/Photo Researchers, Inc.; p. 36, 54 © Telegraph Colour Library/FPG; p. 43 © Nova Stock/Int'l Stock; p. 46 © Giovanni Lunardi/Int'l Stock.

Layout and Design

Thomas Forget

www.ingramcontent.com/pod-product-compliance
Lightning Source LLC
Chambersburg PA
CBHW041113070526
44584CB00002B/159